Stepping on Shadows

Cherrie Taylor

Stepping on Shadows

© Cherrie Taylor

First Edition 2021

Cherrie Taylor has asserted her authorship and given her permission
to Dempsey & Windle for these poems to be published here.

Published by Dempsey & Windle under their VOLE imprint
15 Rosetrees
Guildford
Surrey
GU1 2HS
UK
01483 571164
dempseyandwindle.com

British Library Cataloguing-in-Publication Data

A catalogue record for this book is available from the British Library

ISBN: 978-1-913329-40-2

Cover photo: 'Big Sky'
reproduced by kind permission of Jake Olson Studios (500px.com)

Printed and bound in the UK

For my Mother
whose words I hear everyday
and for my son Dylan with love

Contents

Keep your face
always towards the sunshine –
and shadows will fall
behind you.

Walt Whitman

When you came it was early spring

I remember you brought primroses
    you'd picked from the woods
        just beyond the reach

and the cake in that Coronation tin –
    was made with love   you said
        the recipe you'd found tucked in
        a book of poems

we sat in the garden
    and I brought us tea
        and we ate most of the cake
        I can still taste it

and later we lay together
    and I carried up the last two slices
        and we laughed   we laughed so much

the crumbs I knew we could brush away
    but the chocolate butter icing
        no chance of disguising that

I'll take the sheets home   you said   and you did

I can still see you walking away up the hill
    your red hair flying in the breeze

And when *when* became *then*
    – it's hard to remember
        but I can still smell the primroses
        still taste the cake

Looking up at the window

I see the curtains are closed
how long I wonder
how long until the curtains
are drawn again?

looking again
I see the window
is slightly open
and the curtain is being
lifted in the breeze

it's getting dark now
and I look up again
a chink of light shows
and I see a hand -
like a shadow-play
dancing

I wait below in the shadows
how long I cannot say

the moon sends shafts of light
through the trees
and a silhouette of an owl
is visible on the chimney
above the window

I look up and wait for its call
and I see the window is open
the curtains drawn back
and you lean out

you are wearing the chemise
I gave you and the moon
lights up your face
and your fair hair moves
in the breeze

I step forward
can you see me?
I'm afraid to call out

clouds pass over the moon
light leaves the room
and the window closes
once more

When I was small

the world was
　so much bigger
　　and the gates were wide open

not a single barrier
　barred my way or stopped
　　me exploring the fields and woods
　　　beyond the open gate

not one day passed without
　me seeing　　all there was to see
　　except of course
　　　what was hidden

on that day　　it was the dog
　who knew first　　his low growl
　　and slinky tail

'Here boy,' I said, 'here Jack.'
　but Jack stood back　　beyond
　　the open gate
　　　hackles raised

then I heard
　the shout　the cry　the slap

when I went in I saw
　what had been done...
　　what had been hidden

our dog left first
　I cried when he left
　　the next day we left too

and my world
　became small
　　so much smaller...

"A man stopped near his porch. . ."
from *Train Ride* by Ruth Stone

… the train stalled
and I saw a man
watching from his porch

the talk in
the carriage was of
delays

I waited for the man
to wave
I waved back

the talk went on
only I saw the man
saw the wave

Hotel by the Railroad

(Edward Hopper, 1952)

I keep my eyes lowered   the words a blur
It was a mistake – never return to the same hotel
I just need to get through the next few hours

Small talk over coffee and hash browns   now back in our room...
I would feel more generous to him if he had been kinder

He stands fully clothed except for his jacket
smoking his last cigarette
He gazes into space through the open window
his face as ashen as the wall by the tracks

He's giving a running commentary –
telling me that the whole area has gone downhill
As if I didn't know

I gasped when he lay on me
I hoped it would be a new beginning

He rolled over   too soon... I sensed his sigh
but the sound was drowned out
by the night train from Maine

My silk petticoat fits too well – I know that
... the comment he made
whirls in my head

I would feel more generous if he had been kinder

I bury my head   keep it low
try to concentrate on the words

The book I found in the drawer
Wayward Bride – a dog-eared
Lurid Digest paperback

Three more hours to sit here   to wait
for the next train to Maine

I tell myself
this is the last time...

And what is he thinking
what is he telling himself?

I would feel more generous if he had been kind

Flaxen-haired Child and Green-eyed Dog

Riding fast on a downward path
the flaxen-haired child screams
with delight and the dog with green eyes
and docked tail runs alongside – wagging
the long lost tail. The speeding bike
slows as the train barrier descends
and the front wheel skids to a stop.
The station master blows the whistle
and the 2:45 train to Dormansland
passes in a blur of faces and waves.
No time to stop today. The barrier raised
the flaxen-haired child and the dog
with green eyes and the almost
wagging tail – speed away. First downhill
then climbing the upward path. Ahead is the
farm gate and waiting by the kitchen door
is a flaxen-haired woman. The bike tips up
and the boy falls. No time to cry
for Mummy – no *need* to cry for Mummy.
Come here flaxen-haired boy…
time for tea.

Three Trees

Three trees stood where I now stand
A house – our home stood just there
where low walls and marram slide into sand

I see your face, your eyes – the stare
Flames burn and flare – I hear the crack
read the signs pinned to the rail 'Beware'

Three trees stood here – please bring them back
We were felled too, you say, re opening
the blame – blaming me again – I take the flack

I see a baby's buggy – wheels broken
I see his face in the clouds – tears falling
You look away, say everything, unspoken

The house that was a home is calling
Three trees stood here where now I'm crawling

Ballad of a Hundred Worries
– after a poem by Du Fu (712 – 770 A.D.)

I see him return, my sturdy brown calf –
my husband, who once scaled mountains

And climbed a thousand trees
bringing home everything we needed.

All the food, all the fruit required
and how he placed them on the table.

Where, as a family we sat with happy faces,
said grace, talked, laughed – our children smiling –

Opening the purple dates, sucking on the peaches,
cupping the pears in sticky hands.

I see him look at me as he returns this time,
the house bare as ever and we both know.

We both remember… we are mirror images
we sit at the table – he looks away.

Cryptolepas rhachianecti

my lifestyle does have limits
   I'm stuck to my host   my forehead
      pressed to the back of Jonah's whale

I have no heart-beat but for three days
   I hear two beating hearts   as we ride the storm

no mention of my crusty life – in The Book
   not a word about my eight pairs of feathery *cirre*
      I wave to filter my five a day

no show of reverence to my penis   in body size ratio
   the largest of the animal kingdom

I contain multitudes
– after Walt Whitman

I celebrate myself
    I am the ocean   all the sea creatures

I am a barnacle whose static appearance hides
    my real barnacle life

I am the hermit crab… finding a new home when
    I grow too big

I am a shoal of herring… never to become kippers
    although if I do I will be pleased you enjoy me

I am a dolphin clicking and whistling my echoey waves
    and I'm smiling… so happy since my release

I am the smile on the face of the blue whale
    and the shark with no name

I am a minnow… not wanting to be other fish's breakfast
    but if I must… I will become those fish

I am a seahorse and I take you as a rider and we open the door
    to a new world… taking the old world with us

You will hardly know who I am or what I mean but look for me
    when you open the oyster shell

And if we miss each other
    I will stop somewhere and wait for you

Triton's call…

It all started so slowly
   the change   in texture
      the alteration   transformation
         undulation

looking back was it
   always there   waiting?
      waiting for a moment
         a trigger?

the new bikini perhaps
   or the summer
      when the sea
         never cooled

I look at it now
   so green
      so ultramarine

sitting on this rock
   I look to the shore

part of me longs
   for lazy days
      walking the coastal path
         muddy boots   grazed knees
            cream teas

 I hear
   Triton's
      call…

Not Today

I can't throw you away.
Why not?
I'm only a letter
you never sent.
But I wrote it
to Mum when I was just ten.

I can't throw you away.
Why not?
I'm only a pair of
gloves – so small with fur on
the edge and buttons like eyes.
But my Granny sewed on the fur
and fastened the buttons
I wore them when I was five.

I can't throw you away.
Why not?
I'm only a curl of
hair in a box which has been
closed tight for years.
I know, I'm sorry I've not
looked until now… it's a
lock of my baby hair
kept by my Mum in a
drawer by her bed.

I can't throw you away
not today

I open the drawer…
glasses, little pots of cream
things never seen.

I close the drawer
I'm not sure
I can't decide if I'll
throw you away —
not today

Leaning over the bridge

I catch your reflection
   just for a moment

Is that you? I say
   to the breeze
     Is that you?

she moves on up the River
   taking with her
     the memory

leaning over the bridge   I let a pebble fall
   and watch the ripples circle
     painting a picture

Is that you?   I say
   to the memory

the breeze never listens

breathing in   I close my eyes
  I'm here   you say
    I'm always here

Broken

her small body breaks
my heart screams
I cry for her

her eyes are lost
among the dirt and grime
beneath his plimsoll feet

her gingham dress –
pink and white like mine
still covers her small frame

one leg is bent backwards
an arm is missing
her smile broken

I stoop down and pick her up
he laughs and kicks her arm
along the corridor

I look up into his face
this big boy...
this slayer of my

precious china doll

2 a.m.

I see you through the curtain
looking up
hoping
I will
let
you
in

the doorbell rings
hope presses
harder

the phone rings
my heart beats
faster

our baby wakes
his eyes
look
up

I see you through
the curtain
looking
up

my heart closes the door

"into a strange party..."
from *By Halves* by Fanny Howe

...familiar faces wearing masks step forward
I arrive with Michael who looks like Elvis

the masks slip   we hear a scream
Small Dole girl has hurt her head
who hit her?   who hurt her?
no one asks   everyone knows
he pulls her back   shuts the bedroom door

faceless dancers jive and twist
Dream Lover plays on the Dansette
then auto jumps to *Living Doll*

Party Piece

Don't look at me like that.
Like what?
You know, it's always the same
…the same old tune
I've tried. I've really tried – I have
I have reams of books, notes,
quavers crotchets, scores.
Its hard for me, you don't realise – it's easy for you
Easy – what's with this easy?
Well you just sit there looking grand
your candlesticks facing me
your famous name in gold and black
shouting at me, telling me that
other hands have embraced you,
placed their fingers just so. Go,
pull down your guard – your dust saver
pull back your soft and loud.
Now, now, you're being oversensitive…
pianissimo Cherie!
Don't back pedal – the stool knows, she knows
Für Elise isn't enough for you
and the *Blue Danube* is too blue.

What? What's that you say?

Fortissimo… play
play once more.

Der de der de der de der – da dah dah da…

26

Memento

It used to be on the wall by my bed...
No I don't keep it hidden. I didn't expect you to pry.
You don't understand I loved him.
Don't look at me like that – we all loved him
it wasn't just me. No one talks about his good side.
He was kind. There were others – they were to blame.
Give the book to me. Go! Leave, if you can't hear
what I say – what I remember. I was there after all.
I wanted to marry him. I know he was older
a lot older... but it was my dream.
I talked about it with my parents.
They understood, even though they laughed.
"Our little Ema wants to marry a god!"
I understood much later and of course...
it would have ended in tears. It all ended in tears...
No, he never visited. He never came to our home.
He would have been so welcomed if he had –
he would have loved our dog. She was a pure-bred
like *Blondi*. He would have stroked her and ruffled her coat
like he ruffled my hair. He bent down and took my face
in his hands. His eyes were a beautiful blue – so clear.
Piecing? No, not the eyes I saw. The eyes that smiled
at me – they were honest – big blue eyes like stars.
They were tearful too. I think he knew I loved him.
I was just a child watching him pass by.
My heart leapt with love.
The swastika? Oh that's a keepsake too.

Opening the Secret Drawer

A letter written in her hand – *Dear Frank,*
     the first line – *I'm so sorry...* the last line – *I'm so sorry...*
A sepia photograph dated 1929 – mother and baby girl
A piece of tissue paper folded – inside a golden curl
A little pot of Parma Violets – the smell still sweet
A torn-out section from The London Gazette – giving the date
                         – in 1931 when she changed her name
A legal document of the house purchase in Pinner, Middx.
                                 – both parties named
A Valentine's card – *love you always my darling x*
A tiny notebook with a to-do shopping list on one page:
     bread lard lamb flour sealing wax matches
A book of poems by Ella Wheeler Wilcox –
                        'Solitude' ribbon-marked
A lace handkerchief with the letter *N* hand-embroidered
                               – in the corner
A provisional driving licence dated 1939
A baby's bonnet
A silver vanity mirror – cracked
A folded page from The London Gazette –
     the notice of her untimely death 29th February 1940.
                    And the request – no flowers

James – known as Jim

In Loving Memory of
JAMES ARTHUR BAXTER
Who died July 2nd, 1896
AGED 38 YEARS

~~~

Interred at Newport Pagnell Cemetery, July 5th

'There was a boy whose name was Jim...' Grandma begins, 'his friends were very good to him, they gave him Tea and Cakes and Jam...' I sit next to her with my brother James: we both know how the story ends. James is younger than me, by two years which was a lot then. I was just seven. I squeeze his hand. We both jump when Grandma says, 'Bang!' and thumps her hand on the table. Ponto, the lion was going to eat the boy 'bit by bit.'

As if we weren't frightened enough Grandma would continue with the next story. Matilda – the girl who lied and died in a fire. If the Jim story was aimed at James (he did run away and wouldn't hold hands) Matilda was directed at me. I had told a lie – one little lie but Grandma never let me forget it. I'd taken an extra cake (two iced buns when I was only allowed one). The truth was discovered a week later when it was found at the back of my cupboard, stuck to a party dress. Grandma – like the aunt in the tale, 'kept a Strict Regard for Truth.' Grandma knew the Hillaire Belloc cautionary tales by heart. She would cuddle us after the telling. We wanted to be good to please her.

tea and cakes
and jam
Jim and Matilda
holding hands
with Grandma

Grandma did tell us real family stories as we got older and showed us faded sepia photos. One which fascinated me was of the whole family – all except Great-granddad. The photo shows a horse-drawn trap which followed Great-granddad's coffin. Grandma's brother Arthur stands in front of the horse holding the bridle. Great-grandma Susan is in the centre standing by the trap's large wheels. Grandma aged seven years is sitting in it with her four older sisters and baby brother Jim. They are all dressed in black with large hats.

Great-granddad bled to death in a field: died on the earth he had been ploughing, his leg caught in the blades. His name was James – known as Jim. Grandma read us the wording on his memorial card, and then the poem that accompanied it:–

How soon my life was ended
And hastened to decay;
An accident befell me
Which took my life away.

Grandma kept these mementoes locked in a metal box under her bed.

James known
as Jim
memories
more than dust
held in a tin

In her smile... I see my smile.

This photograph was taken on the day of my great-grandfather's funeral, July 1896. My grandma, 'Ninna' sits at the back.

It Couldn't Happen Here...
— after Cavafy

I can hear them coming
No that's the wind
They're not here yet, not yet.

The power was down.
We had known for weeks
We'll stay, I sighed. We'll stay.

I didn't know we'd all be leaving
that the *Barbarians* would come –
it couldn't happen here...

We'd watched others pass by...
It's only a matter of time,
It's only a matter of time.

But it doesn't happen here
I heard you say over and over
again – over and over again.

It will be fine, we'll be fine-
pack our clothes and photos
put them in plastic – plastic bags.

Put your teddies in your school bags
Shall we wear our arm bands?
And bring our blow-up crocodile?

How many are leaving?
Our street and all the streets
down to the sea.

It doesn't happen here...
Come, come, quick, quick –
the *Barbarians* are coming

.   We spill our way
like hundreds and thousands
to the shore
to the jetty
and wait.

In Reply to Germain, Who Visited My Green Shuttered House by The Sea When I Wasn't There to Greet Him
— *after Wang Wei (699 – 759 A.D.)*

I live alone along the coastal path
where sea meets sky.

When you parked your car by the church
and walked up the narrow chalky path

who opened the gate and said, come in?
Who looked into your eyes and said, hello?

Did you see the garden – the thrift, the tamarisk?
Did you notice the thistles, the nettles?

Did they bite and sting? And when the weatherboards
stuttered, did the house smile? Did the shutters rattle?

Were the guillemots shouting their song? Was the cormorant
sitting – as cormorants do – shaking her coat?

And as the clouds gathered around you and the sky fell,
surely you heard the singing and listened to the bells.

Stepping on Shadows

I watch from my window
it's dark outside
the moon is the only light

Is that you?
your hair the colour of stardust

Is that you – your smile?
clouds eclipse my view

Closer now...
you step back on your shadow
and look up

I watch from my window
it's dark outside
your smile is the only light

Leaving the shadows
you open the gate
I watch... I wait

A candle burns in the room of rain...

Baby Ceri is two weeks old
  Carman the German Shepherd sits by her crib
    the condition is clear to the medical team

her body is perfect   her tiny face shows a faraway look
  not slack-jawed   no simple stare
    no webbed feet   she has ten fingers   ten toes

I watch as her father picks her up
  holds her like a delicate flower to his chest
    her nose is an upturned button   she breathes a gentle sigh

her profile shows us   the back of her head is flat
  where her father cups his hand
    half of Ceri's brain is missing

for weeks they tend her flame
  I watch as hope rises and falls
    rises and falls...

they keep a twist of her golden hair
  a candle burns *in the room of rain*

you'd know her house by the drawn blinds...

what happiness is

have I been a good son? tell me
you are a good son – you are

have I been a good brother? tell me
you are a good brother – you are

why did you leave me brother?
why did you leave me? tell me

I thought… I thought you were there…
I thought you were there with me
with me when Heaven fell

my brother
my brother

I have forgotten what happiness is

Mass exodus
Delhi, March 30th 2020

In small groups and large crowds
they leave through inner-city lanes
down interstate highways

Lock-down no work
no money for food
no money for rent

'We have to go back
to our village,' Rekha says,
she holds her son's hand

Amrta is ten – almost a man
'How far is it?' he asks, 'how many days?'
'It's a long way… many days.'

Her husband Amar carries
their little girl
Lata sleeps in his arms

An elderly women is a few steps behind –
Rekha calls to her mother '*Maji* keep up.'

'We haven't eaten for two days,' Rekha says,
'We are scared of the virus but hunger will kill us.'

Line upon line of walkers
with scarfs and masks over their mouths
tattered duffel bags spilling clothes
blankets, pots and pans

Rekha's mother trails behind
The family stop and wait

Amrta walks back
'*Naniji* keep up.'

What's that got to do with the price of chips?

Chips. The image was unbidden. It was there for all to see – if they looked. If they could bear to look. I looked. I can still see the chips. The scene. The setting. The image returns… unbidden.

I love chips. When I was a child my friend and I used to walk down the road where we lived to buy chips. I was about six or seven years old. We'd cross the railway line on a footbridge called Jacob's Ladder. It didn't have a sign that said Jacob's Ladder, but we all knew it was called Jacob's Ladder. On the other side of the bridge was a fish and chip shop – it's still there and we bought a penny's worth of chips in a little bag. It was an old penny. A big old penny with the Queen's head on it or maybe it was the King's head. We'd queue up and get a penny bag of chips and the lady behind the counter would add a sprinkle of salt and pour on some vinegar. She would give us each a square of newspaper so the chips didn't burn our hands and we'd eat the chips as we crossed back over the bridge. We did this for years but each year when new potatoes were dug the price would go up. And it would be two pennies. Two big round brown pennies and the next year three pennies and I can remember it going up as far as sixpence – a silver sixpenny piece. But they were still in little bags about the same size. The size may have increased slightly but not much. We'd eat them with our fingers. These days you get little wooden forks. Fingers are best and licking them afterwards. What was really good about the little bags was that the vinegar would stay in the bottom and make the chips taste even better and we'd tip the bag up – so not to waste a drop.

I still love chips. But eating them from little bags and newspaper is a thing of the past. These days they come in a polystyrene tray. A white polystyrene tray. A soulless white polystyrene tray.

Unbidden... the image returns

sitting
cross-legged
outside Tesco Express   asleep face-down
in a tray of chips...
chips down

I bring you daffodils
(Arles, France)

I want to sit with you in your Yellow House
in eighteen hundred and eighty-eight.

I bring you daffodils. A new subject – still yellow.
I set up a still life. Cloud-like to stop your wanderings.

I send Paul away to stop tempers flaring. He scowls
but I insist. "Life is on a razor's edge."

I busy myself emptying vases of empty heads,
ask "What is it, Vincent, about sunflowers?"

"Their faces dance in my head – it's an obsession."
A single tear slides down his face, painting his stubble blue.

I take his hand and we walk to the market to buy fresh peaches
and croissants "My treat." I say, knowing Theo's cheque is late.

Sitting now in the yellow room in the Yellow House
I open a bottle of red, "Is this okay for breakfast?" I ask.

"Its fine but I'll just have one glass." He smiles. He spends
the day painting the daffodils and I recite Wordsworth.

"I remember William," he says. "He visited me once
with Dorothy. I wanted to paint her but she was too shy."

We stroll out on a warm sunset, breathing in evening air.
I look at him – he's calm, composed. I knew I was right to come.

We get back to the Yellow House and he sleeps in the yellow bed.
I sit on the yellow chair reciting 'Daffodils'.

I stroke his head and cup my hands over his ears.
He opens his eyes. "I wish…" he says. "I wish too," I say.

No one interviewed the bird
after *Flannon Isle* by Wilfred Wilson Gibson

Three men dwelt on Flannon Isle
to keep the lamp alight
then one December night
the lamp went out...

The lighthouse keepers were never found
the black sun-blister'd door was open wide
a table spread with meat and cheese and bread.

No sign of life except a feeble cheep
from a caged bird   her foot chained to the perch.

No one interviewed the bird.

She was given into my care   her leg unleashed
...for days I tempted her with insects seeds and fruit
she opened her beak – I drip fed her tepid water
watched her regain strength   start to speak.

I listened at first   not wanting to pressure
or press her into talking   to say too much.
Her first words gave me her name
'My name is Molly' and as if I had not heard
she said again 'My name is Molly the Myna bird.'

As the days passed I informed
the investigation team that Molly had spoken.

No one wished to interview the bird.

I showed Molly faded photographs
of the three lighthouse keepers
Thomas, James and Donald
and looked for signs   responses
clues to her emotion.

She knew each man's name
pronounced them with a Scottish burr
she cocked her head side to side
pecked the sepia faces

She was gentle when I showed her James and Tom
but when she saw Donald she screeched
tore at his face and repeated in a frenzy
'Donald begone! Donald begone! Donald begone!'

No one interviewed the bird.

Swinging Sixties – Sweaty Betty
(July 2018)

where's Jimmy?
where's John?
they've gone
it's not the same

the *Shakespeare's Head*
is still on the corner
but the *Bag O'Nails*
where Linda met Paul
– closed for good   gone

the iconic neon sign –
W*elcoming the World*
has gone   replaced
– no welcome
it's not the same

The Sex Pistols
The Jam   The Kinks
their faces mist in the
heat haze

those *dedicated*
followers of fashion
no longer wear
polka-dots or frilly panties
it's not the same

The Rolling Stones
rolled over
rocked back in 2012
(it wasn't the same)

where's Mary Quant?
where's Pam Hogg?
where are the Mods?
they've gone

the voices
the spirit is dead
the scent of patchouli
bombed out by *Lush*

30 °C and rising...
I'll meet you in the
Shakespeare's Head   you said

arriving at eleven
you're at the bar
your flares and your hair
are the same...
you look old
you look faded
– you were fixed
in the sixties
now your eyes
are *dead*

I buy you a drink
and move on...

Sweaty Betty beckons
fitness food and fashion
not dedicated
may be interesting
won't be swinging

it's not the same.

Suppose

Suppose I could come back
and join you again
turn back the clock
unfold the cloth of time

become conjoined
end this twin-ship
skip back into space
complete the jigsaw.

Suppose. Oh! Suppose...
instead of looking at each other
we were *one* again... would we
adjust or would you fuss
and wobble as you did before?

I've kept you stable,
pulled you back from
bouncing around
kept you grounded
Obliquity – I think...
the scientists call
what I gave you.

But I'm sad, I'm pale –
you're blue – I can tell
and when I try to discuss it
with the others, well...

The Red Planet doesn't understand
he sees us as equals in size and The Sun –
well... she's ninety three million miles away –
don't let's discuss it with her.

I orbit you once every twenty eight days
and I gaze down – mourning for
what I have lost.

Cars Confetti Ice & Mars Bars

the bus stops at Upper Parliament Street, I cut through
the walkway to Grafton. the sun lights up the broken glass.

the streets are quiet, deserted, it's a school day. no cars parked
except burnt out shells, skeletons with broken glass

windscreens. a Liverbird dangles like a dream catcher.
tenement windows at street level see nothing, their eyes mask
                                                         broken glass.

the silence is broken by a distant sound, a faint blast from the Ferry
drifts on the wind. I feel shards under my feet, broken glass

fragments of confetti ice, embedded into the cracks.
no trees or flowers, the only colours that glisten, broken glass.

broken bottles speak of no returns, no money back
from the corner shop, its boarded-up windows remember broken glass,

now blinded by hardboard, mesh grills and padlocks,
doors reinforced with metal plates. no more broken glass.

graffiti on the walls speak the unspeakable. inside the people
are friendly, their smiles not dampened by the gloom or broken glass.

the woman at the checkout hands me a Mars Bar with the quip
'helping you work rest *and* play!' I smile. the broken glass

jars. I am broken, broken-hearted. this is the summer of '73
& Cherrie's colours need to shine. at Lime Street Station
                                       I say *ta ra* to broken glass.

The Long Woman

– after woodcuts by Eric Ravilious

Come away with me   you say
showing me places   tempting me
to walk your way

the road is too long   I say
the houses too small
the garden has shade   you say

I can only see drakes and serpents
owls and wingèd beasts and clouds
with curly-hornèd rams

I will shelter you   you say
tame the beasts   bring back the sun
make a bed beneath the tree

you take my hand   it turns to stone
I lift my staff and walk away
dragging the chalk beneath my feet

Aquilina Waits
(Arundel:53 AD)

The River Tarrant forms a wide tidal estuary and close to the waterfront stands a large Roman Villa. Aquilina a young Roman girl knows it is her time. She is thinking of the young man who she loves. Word has come that he has returned to southern Britain. His journey will take him on the Roman Road from Noviomagus to Arundel – a road well-travelled. Aquilina prays that he will find his way to the Villa… She has to get a message to him.

Aquilina opens the
tablet and writes
his name in wax
Thracius
the stylus slips

Thracius travels along
the valley at Binsted Brook
so near now to Arundel
he feels his
worries return

the way
to the Villa
is marked
will Aquilina still
be waiting?

Aquilina sees him
in the distance
the baby cries
she holds him
to her breast

Thracius has brought with him a gold Bulla amulet which he places gently around the tiny boy's neck. Albus looks up – his dark eyes mirror those of his father. Thracius and Aquilina embrace and walk west towards the Villa.

Aquilina's father Drusus
is seated in the atrium
who is this Thracius –
father of Albus!
Drusus waits…

All Roads…

We stroll along
Stane Street – you
in your Roman garb
me in my bikini

You'll need to cover up
if we meet him – you
say in a language I've
yet to learn

Antoninus Pius – you mean?
I say – applying more sunscreen -
he's pretty open-minded
didn't he bathe naked with Medusa?

You give me that *turned to stone* look -
I'm more concerned, he continues
about Caracalla the Hoody
I hear he waits in Noviomagus

By The Cross – Oh no sweat!
I'll nip in the Cathedral
don a cassock or piece
together a dress from Jigsaw

Is that near Costa?
my Roman runner asks.
Just opposite I say,
in a language he's learning fast,
I'll get you a Skinny Latte
or would you like a Mocha?

You have a Mocha
if you like – mine's a
Caffé Corretto with a
shot of Sambuca

He hands me a coin
Antoninus Pius dupondius
my treat he says – with a
smile we both understand

We wander down
West Street – you
in your Roman garb
me in my bikini

Arundel River Walk

tanka sequence

opaque water
reflecting trees and sky
a moorhen
and I
meet eye to eye

castle walls
keeping
history locked away
no flag for a baby
born today

white swan
foraging
selects tasty leaves
from the bank
her insights revealed

castle in the stream
where mallards rest
turret walls
that cannot trap:
they swim away

yellow and brown
round bright spot on leaf
not meant to be…
insect? disease?
perfect study for painting

Hard times

half –
light
then the
gentle tap
on the window starts
the day   Knocker-Upper tap taps

I
look
down and
meet his eyes
rub my eyes and give
a thank-you wave   hard times await

little
one
wakes   the
coughing starts
I soothe her head and
wait   the whooping stops   her eyes close

we
know
we both
know the signs
it's gone on   too long…
the hyssop and honey syrup –

we
hope
will help…
I kiss her
goodbye   morning breaks…
sixteen hour day   hard times await

Haiku

darkness brings tears
seeking light...
I reach for your hand

                puddles deepen
                children's laughter
                splashes

field of blue
red poppy
waving

The House of Torn Souls

*In memory of the murdered victims
of Fred and Rosemary West.*

I

Ordinary

We did stuff, just ordinary stuff.
Day trips to Bristol Zoo in the van,
squish-squashed like sardines in a can.
Those caged monkeys had nothing on us,
we had freedom, we did ordinary stuff.

On Guy Fawkes Night we'd head into town,
snaking, hand in hand towards
the loudest bangs. Dad in the front
with Heather held high – her fear frozen
in time – she clung to him, was one with him. Bang!

We did stuff, yes, ordinary stuff.
We had trips to the Malverns, to
the Forest of Dean – look see our snaps,
watch this video clip – we're smiling.
We're all smiling. We did ordinary stuff.

Our garden was like an orchard once.
Candy floss confetti fell like whispers
on our faces, as we lay down
dreamlike on beds of grass. Innocent
of sharper blades and stuff to come.

We did stuff. Oh. Ordinary stuff.
Parties and barbecues. Dad took charge.
Rose got the ketchup – don't spill nowt,
she said, as we rocked to and fro, to
and fro on the crazed patio to and fro.

We dressed and undressed our paper dolls,
teaching them the wicked witches way
with cuddles and smacks on bare bums.
They crackled and crumpled then said,
it's okay, and smiled – in an ordinary way.

II.

My Dad the Ice Cream Man

My Dad had an ice cream van and
when I was a baby I slept

under the counter and when I
cried he played *Greensleeves.*

III.

Come in the Garden Close the Gate

Come in the garden close the gate,
'Beware of the Bear' sign has gone.
Tread softly. Listen, I can wait.

Our Wendy house sorrow reshaped
paper dolls into black swans.
Come in the garden close the gate.

Evacuate the bruised landscape –
excavate the patio pond.
Tread softly. Listen, I can wait.

My jigsaw bone puzzle awaits
resurrection from Babylon.
Come in the garden close the gate.

My ring, my soul, it's not too late,
please look for my toes on the lawn.
Tread softly. Listen, I can wait.

Got my O-Levels, got a date.
Retie the threads, colour crayon
me in – open the garden gate.
Tread softly. Listen – I can't wait.

IV.

My Dad the Builder

My Dad was a builder and I
was his mate. *Fred West & Daughter*

he called us. His customers loved
his charm and me on his arm.

V.

If You Sit Very Still

If you sit very still and close your eyes
you can hear the sun move...

Tread softly as you open the gate,
touch the new day with baby steps.

Great Peter rings out as we pass the
Cathedral – pealing the way down to
Eastgate. Holding hands we cut through
Hampton Way and here we are…
in Cromwell Street.

A feral wind bites our faces -
we wrap our wings tighter.
I can smell the blossoms, you say.
I still taste the fear.

There are more of us now, shadowed hallows,
seventies mannequins frozen in time.
I steady myself and like a Blue Badge
automaton – I lead the way.

Ignore the pyracantha sentinels
guarding the walkway with their firethorn knives.
Let the crisp-bag leaves wave you past
the warning signs, 'No Public Drinking.'
Blink back the graffiti…
Kick aside the battered Stella cans which,
like defiant symbols, join the parade.

Sixteen black bollards stand to attention.
Seventh-day Adventists vie to be heard -
proclaiming, 'Peace and Sanity in a Mad, Mad World.'

… the digging stopped on the Seventh-day,
cold comfort to the living, who like them
were blind to the carnage at *Twenty Five*.

The house of torn souls is torn down,
excised from our town – the absence yells...

But look down the twitten, look, look and listen
the violets are growing, innocent of those
who cried beneath.

There's no-one home but I'm with you today.
And I wipe your tears and weave votive offerings,
made from spiders' webs and leaves of Heartsease.

And we place them where apple
blossoms fell from the trees. And I say,
shall we close our eyes and sit very still…
so we can hear the sun move? And
you say… *Please.*

VI.

My Dad's Fish

My Dad loved his tropical fish and
when he was locked away he'd say

with watery eyes – Are they okay?
His fish didn't pine.

Notes and Links

'Into a strange party' – Small Dole is a village in West Sussex

'A candle burns in the room of rain' – inspired by the poem *At Roane Head* by Robin Robertson

'What happiness is' – Syrian refugee Mohammad Alhajali was the first named victim of the Grenfell Tower fire. His brother Omar said in his last phone call, Mohammad asked if he'd been a good son and brother, and requested forgiveness from his family.

'Mass Exodus (Delhi March 2020)' – I wrote this poem after listening to an interview on Al Jazeera, with a family – one of thousands who had to leave the city after the Covid 19 lockdown. The names have been changed. https://www.aljazeera.com/news/2020/03/coronavirus-lockdown-india-grapples-migrant-workers-exodus-200328151304900.html

'James – known as Jim' – James Baxter was my Great-grandfather.

'Aquilina Waits (Arundel: 53 AD)' Excavations in Arundel, West Sussex in 1983 revealed evidence of a very large, first-century Roman Villa – close to the waterfront at the western end of Tarrant Street. Some of the finds from this excavation are held in Arundel Museum. A metal writing stylus was found and can be seen in a display cabinet. The River Arun was known in Celtic times as Trisantona (Tarrant)

'The House of Torn Souls' – this sequence of poems formed part of a final examination in 2015 with the Open University – Advanced Creative Writing – where poetry was my chosen option. I undertook extensive research into the difficult subject of the murders committed by Fred and Rosemary West over 20 years and the discovery of the bodies in 1994. I had access to video and audio recordings and archived material. I visited the city of Gloucester as part of this project.

Acknowledgements

Acknowledgements are due to the editors of magazines and anthologies in which some of these poems were first published: *Reach Poetry, Coast Lines (West Sussex Writers: 2017) An Anthology (Shoreham Wordfest 2020)*

I would like to thank Sarah Higbee for her support and encouragement with my writing over the last ten years. Sarah opened my eyes to poetry and the different poetic forms.

And a big thank-you to Mandy Pannett for shining a special light and encouraging my creativity.

Thanks also to John McCulloch (New Writing South) He widened my world view of poetry and set me new challenges.

I am grateful to the organisers and members of River poets (Arundel) and West Sussex Writers, for their continued support and encouragement.

Lastly a very big thank you to Geoffrey Winch who has been a mentor and guide.

Cherrie Taylor was born in Cornwall and moved to West Sussex when aged five. The coast has always been important to her, and some of her first words were written in the sand!

Having written stories and poetry since childhood, in 2012 she studied Creative Writing with the Open University in order to develop her techniques. Her influences are wide-ranging and her work has been published in *Coast Lines* (West Sussex Writers, 2018), *Shoreham Wordfest Anthology* (2020), and *Reach Poetry*. She has also been the winner of two poetry competitions .

Her poems always have a poignancy which, in the main, empathise with human concerns, often profoundly but at other times light-heartedly; and she never shies away from tackling 'difficult' subjects by ensuring her researches are well-founded.